Finding Hope When Life Seems Dark

KAY ARTHUR
PETE DE LACY

HARVEST HOUSE PUBLISHERS

EUGENE, OREGON

Unless otherwise indicated, all Scripture quotations are taken from the New American Standard Bible®, © 1960, 1962, 1963, 1968, 1971, 1972, 1973, 1975, 1977, 1995 by The Lockman Foundation. Used by permission. (www.Lockman.org)

Verses marked KJV are taken from the King James Version of the Bible.

Cover by Koechel Peterson & Associates, Inc., Minneapolis, Minnesota

FINDING HOPE WHEN LIFE SEEMS DARK
Copyright © 2006 by Precept Ministries International
Published by Harvest House Publishers
Eugene, Oregon 97402
www.harvesthousepublishers.com

Library of Congress Cataloging-in-Publication Data
Arthur, Kay, 1933-
  Finding hope when life seems dark / Kay Arthur and Pete De Lacy.
      p. cm.—(The new inductive study series)
  ISBN-13: 978-0-7369-1825-1 (pbk.)
  ISBN-10: 0-7369-1825-6 (pbk.)
  1. Bible. O.T. Minor prophets—Study and teaching. I. De Lacy, Pete. II. Title. III. Series.
BS1560.A78 2006
224'.90071—dc22   2006001335

Printed in the United States of America

06 07 08 09 10 11 12 13 14 / BP-CF / 10 9 8 7 6 5 4 3 2 1

CONTENTS

∽∽∽∽∽

How to Get Started...

Reading directions is sometimes difficult and hardly ever enjoyable! Most often you just want to get started. Only if all else fails will you read the instructions. We understand, but please don't approach this study that way. These brief instructions are a vital part of getting started on the right foot! These few pages will help you immensely.

FIRST

As you study Hosea, Micah, Nahum, Habakkuk, and Zephaniah, you will need four things in addition to this book:

1. A Bible that you are willing to mark in. The marking is essential. An ideal Bible for this purpose is *The New Inductive Study Bible (NISB)*. The *NISB* is in a single-column text format with large, easy-to-read type, which is ideal for marking. The margins of the text are wide and blank for note taking.

The *NISB* also has instructions for studying each book of the Bible, but it does not contain any commentary on the text, nor is it compiled from any theological stance. Its purpose is to teach you how to discern truth for yourself through the inductive method of study. (The various charts and maps that you will find in this study guide are taken from the *NISB*).

Whichever Bible you use, just know you will need to mark in it, which brings us to the second item you will need…

2. A fine-point, four-color ballpoint pen or various colored fine-point pens that you can use to write in your Bible. Office supply stores should have these.

3. Colored pencils or an eight-color leaded Pentel pencil.

4. A composition book or a notebook for working on your assignments or recording your insights.

SECOND

1. As you study these five minor prophets, you will be given specific instructions for each day's study. These should take you between 20 and 30 minutes a day, but if you spend more time than this, you will increase your intimacy with the Word of God and the God of the Word.

If you are doing this study in a class and you find the lessons too heavy, simply do what you can. To do a little is better than to do nothing. Don't be an all-or-nothing person when it comes to Bible study.

Remember, anytime you get into the Word of God, you enter into more intensive warfare with the devil (our enemy). Why? Every piece of the Christian's armor is related to the Word of God. And our one and only offensive weapon is the sword of the Spirit, which is the Word of God. The enemy wants you to have a dull sword. Don't cooperate! You don't have to!

2. As you read each chapter, train yourself to ask the "5 W's and an H": who, what, when, where, why, and how. Asking questions like these helps you see exactly what the Word of God is saying. When you interrogate the text with the 5 W's and an H, you ask questions like these:

a. **What** is the chapter about?

b. **Who** are the main characters?

c. **When** does this event or teaching take place?

d. **Where** does this happen?

e. **Why** is this being done or said?

f. **How** did it happen?

3. The "when" of events or teachings is very important and should be marked in an easily recognizable way in your Bible. You could mark it with a clock (like the one shown here) in the margin of your Bible beside the verse where the time phrase occurs. You may want to underline or color the references to time in one specific color.

4. You will be given certain key words to mark throughout these five Old Testament books. This is the purpose of the colored pencils and the colored pens. If you will develop the habit of marking your Bible in this way, you will find it will make a significant difference in the effectiveness of your study and in how much you remember.

A **key word** is an important word that the author uses repeatedly in order to convey his message to his reader. Certain key words will show up throughout each book; others will be concentrated in specific chapters or segments of a book. When you mark a key word, you should also mark its synonyms (words that mean the same thing in the context) and any pronouns *(he, his, she, her, it, we, they, us, our, you, their, them)* in the same way you have marked the key word. We will give you suggestions for ways to mark key words in your daily assignments.

You can use colors or symbols or a combination of colors and symbols to mark words for easy identification. However, colors are easier to distinguish than symbols. When we use symbols, we keep them very simple. For example, you could color *repent* yellow but put a red diagram like this over it repent because it indicates a change of mind.

When marking key words, mark them in a way that is easy for you to remember.

If you devise a color-coding system for marking key words throughout your Bible, then when you look at the pages of your Bible, you will see instantly where a key word is used.

You might want to make yourself a bookmark listing the words you want to mark along with their colors and/or symbols.

5. AT A GLANCE charts are located at the end of each book's study. As you complete your study of each chapter, record the main theme of that chapter under the appropriate chapter number. The main theme of a chapter is what the chapter deals with the most. It may be an event or a particular subject or teaching.

If you will fill out the AT A GLANCE charts as you progress through the study, you will have a complete synopsis of the books when you are finished. If you have a *New Inductive Study Bible,* you will find the same charts in your Bible (pages 1453, 1499, 1506, 1514, and 1522). If you record your chapter themes there, you'll have them for a ready reference.

6. Always begin your study with prayer. As you do your part to handle the Word of God accurately, you must remember that the Bible is a divinely inspired book. The words that you are reading are truth, given to you by God so you can know Him and His ways more intimately. These truths are divinely revealed.

> For to us God revealed them through the Spirit; for the Spirit searches all things, even the depths of God. For who among men knows

the thoughts of a man except the spirit of the
man which is in him? Even so the thoughts of
God no one knows except the Spirit of God
(1 Corinthians 2:10-11).

Therefore ask God to reveal His truth to you as He leads
and guides you into all truth. He will if you will ask.

7. Each day when you finish your lesson, meditate on
what you saw. Ask your heavenly Father how you should
live in light of the truths you have just studied. At times,
depending on how God has spoken to you through His
Word, you might even want to record these "Lessons for
Life" in the margin of your Bible next to the text you have
studied. Simply put "LFL" in the margin of your Bible and
then, as briefly as possible, record the lesson for life that you
want to remember.

THIRD

This study is set up so that you have an assignment for
every day of the week—so that you are in the Word daily.
If you work through your study in this way, you will find
it more profitable than doing a week's study in one sitting.
Pacing yourself this way allows time for thinking through
what you learn on a daily basis!

The seventh day of each week differs from the other six
days. The seventh day is designed to aid group discussion;
however, it's also profitable if you are studying this book
individually.

The "seventh" day is whatever day in the week you
choose to finish your week's study. On this day, you will
find a verse or two for you to memorize and STORE IN YOUR
HEART. Then there is a passage to READ AND DISCUSS. This
will help you focus on a major truth or major truths covered
in your study that week.

To assist those using the material in a Sunday school class or a group Bible study, there are QUESTIONS FOR DISCUSSION OR INDIVIDUAL STUDY. Even if you are not doing this study with anyone else, answering these questions would be good for you.

If you are in a group, be sure every member of the class, including the teacher, supports his or her answers and insights from the Bible text itself. Then you will be handling the Word of God accurately. As you learn to see what the text says and compare Scripture with Scripture, the Bible explains itself.

Always examine your insights by carefully observing the text to see what it *says*. Then, before you decide what the passage of Scripture *means*, make sure that you interpret it in the light of its context. Scripture will never contradict Scripture. If it ever seems to contradict the rest of the Word of God, you can be certain that something is being taken out of context. If you come to a passage that is difficult to understand, reserve your interpretations for a time when you can study the passage in greater depth.

The purpose of the THOUGHT FOR THE WEEK is to share with you what we consider to be an important element in your week of study. We have included it for your evaluation and, hopefully, for your edification. This section will help you see how to walk in light of what you learned.

Books in The New Inductive Study Series are survey courses. If you want to do a more in-depth study of a particular book of the Bible, we suggest you do a Precept Upon Precept Bible study course on that book. You may obtain more information on these courses by contacting Precept Ministries International at 800-763-8280, visiting our website at www.precept.org, or filling out and mailing the response card in the back of this book.

FINDING HOPE WHEN LIFE SEEMS DARK

In 2005, hurricane Katrina slammed into the Gulf coast of the United States with the most devastating winds, high tides, and torrential rains we had seen for more than 40 years. Coastal cities in Louisiana, Mississippi, and Alabama lay directly in its path—including New Orleans, which is below sea level but is protected by levees designed to keep the waters of the Mississippi River and Lake Pontchartrain from flooding the city.

Authorities warned residents to evacuate, but many stayed. When the storm passed, life seemed dark. The levees failed, and much of the city was underwater. The wind had destroyed thousands of square miles of houses and businesses in three states. People were without electricity or drinking water; roads and railroads were destroyed; hundreds of people were missing and dead; and there seemed to be no way to distribute food, water, and health-care supplies or to provide basic public safety services.

Tens of thousands of people were trying to survive in these dire circumstances. For many, this was the darkest hour they had ever experienced. They lost everything—homes, possessions, loved ones, dignity...hope. Who would rescue them from this nightmare? What could be done?

Where were the relief agencies? Who would rescue them from this almost unbelievable squalor—and when?

Life seemed dark; where would they find hope?

In the years between Solomon's reign as King of Israel and the Babylonian captivity, Israel was living in spiritual and moral squalor. The "levees" who might have held back a flood of evil—the prophets, priests, kings, and princes—had failed; idolatry had overflowed the land, and the nation was awash in idols from adjacent nations and cultures. The waters were rising, and the people were about to drown without realizing it. They would not find safety in their houses, even though most of the popular prophets said everything would be all right.

Would the people listen to these *false* prophets, whose promises of security had dulled the nation's sensibilities, or would they turn instead to God's *holy* prophets, who would faithfully give them His word of truth? When life seemed dark, would the people choose truth in order to find hope?

God sent these prophets to warn His people to flee from idolatry. If Israel ignored them, He said, they would be destroyed, taken captive, ripped out of the land of their inheritance. He would judge them in many ways but *always* with the purpose of turning them back to Him—always calling them to repair the breach, rebuild the walls, and restore the kingdom to righteousness and true worship so they wouldn't perish. Judgment was always mingled with the promise of hope.

They would find their hope in Him…if they would only listen.

A BRIEF BACKGROUND FOR STUDYING THE PROPHETS

In the Bible, we find two kinds of prophets: those whose spoken messages became parts of the historical books of the Bible (like Elisha and Elijah) and those whose messages became whole books of the Bible (like Isaiah and Jonah). The Old Testament of the Christian Bible includes four "major prophets" and twelve "minor prophets." *Major* and *minor* refer to the length and significance of the books.

The minor prophets fall into two groups: preexilic and postexilic, depending on whether they ministered before or after the exile of the southern kingdom (Judah) to Babylon from 605 to 536 BC. In this booklet, we'll study five of the nine preexilic prophets: Hosea, Micah, Nahum, Habakkuk, and Zephaniah. You can learn about the rest of the preexilic prophets (Joel, Obadiah, Amos, and Jonah) in *Discovering the God of Second Chances*. The three postexilic prophets (Haggai, Zechariah, and Malachi) are the subject of *Opening the Windows of Blessing*. Both of those study guides are included in the New Inductive Study Series.

When King Solomon died, the Israelites divided into two nations—Israel in the north and Judah in the south. Israel led the way into idolatry, and despite periods of revival, Judah also played the harlot with the gods of other nations.

The five prophets we will study in this booklet address both the northern and southern kingdoms.

Though God commissioned His prophets to preach unique messages to different audiences, He gave them a common theme—hope when life seems dark. That theme is for all people in all times. Your life may seem dark right now. Maybe you can't hear God's voice or see His hand guiding you, or maybe you even wonder if He has abandoned you. God's people through the centuries have struggled with these same feelings, and as we see how God provided for them, we can learn from them and trust God to provide for us now.

As you study these prophets, who spoke God's message of hope to His people, we pray that you too will find hope.

Hosea

INTRODUCTION TO HOSEA

~~~~~~

In 931 BC, the kingdom of Israel was ripped in half. The southern kingdom, Judah, was composed of two tribes, Judah and Benjamin, plus a few members of other tribes who remained faithful to the temple service in Jerusalem. The northern kingdom, Israel (consisting of ten tribes), created its own worship system of idols and priests. For almost 200 years, God raised up prophets to turn Israel away from idolatry and back to Him. Around 755 BC, He sent one last prophet to Israel—Hosea.

Israel had played the harlot, committing spiritual adultery with the gods of other nations. What message would God give Hosea to show them their sin? What method would God use to turn them back to Him?

Jezreel - For Yet A little while

Lo-ruhanah - (Daughter): For I will no more have mercy.

Lo-Ammi - For you are not my people

I Will - Avenge The blood of Jezreel upon The House Jehu
I will - Break The bow of Ireal in The Valley or Jezreel
I will - no more have mercy upon The house of Isreal
I will - utterly Take Then Away
I will have mercy upon The house of Tudah
I will not be your God.

16

A WIFE OF HARLOTRY

Would you select a wife you knew was going to practice prostitution? A wife who would be unfaithful to her vows, who would go after other men? And *have children* with them?

DAY ONE

Read Hosea 1 and underline each phrase that mentions the Lord speaking to Hosea.

Read Hosea 1 again and note the names of kings. Compare them to the ones listed on THE RULERS AND PROPHETS OF HOSEA'S TIME on page 18. This will help you see the historical setting of this book.

Note the names of Hosea's children and any marginal notes that interpret the names. What reasons does the text give for the children's names?

DAY TWO

Now read through the chapter again and mark every reference to *harlotry*[1] with a red cloud like this—harlotry—and  underline the phrase *I will.*

THE RULERS AND PROPHETS OF HOSEA'S TIME

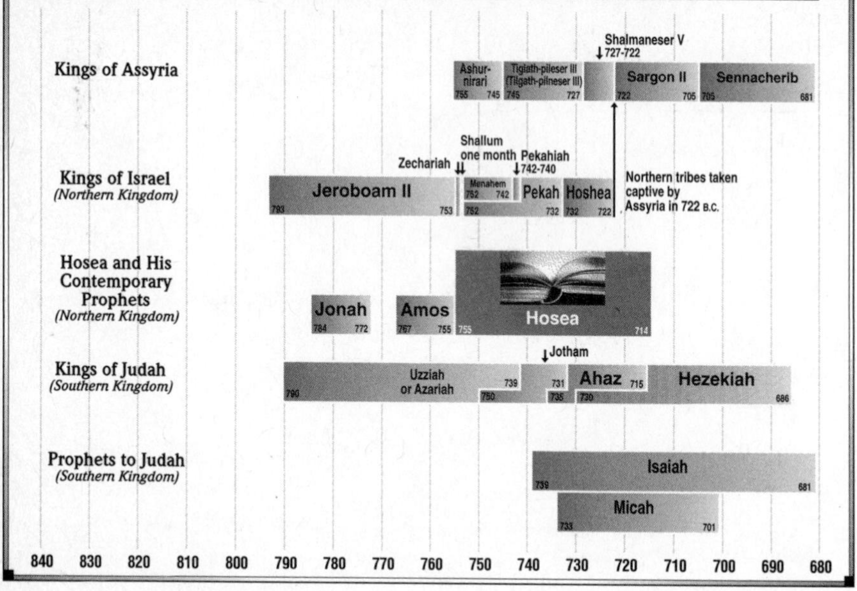

Because The Land commited great whoredom, departing from The Lord.

Why did God tell Hosea to marry a harlot?

Who's behind all the "I will's"? List the actions this phrase introduces. God

Notice the first word of verse 10. How does the tone of the chapter shift there? What does God say in verses 10 and 11? Yet

Read Genesis 22:17-18; Ezekiel 37:21-24; and Romans 9:22-26. What does Hosea 1:10-11 mean?

What practical expressions of hope can you find in this chapter? That God Keeps his Promises

Think through the chapter and determine the theme of this chapter—the main topic, point, or message—and record it on HOSEA AT A GLANCE on page 61.

DAY THREE

Read Hosea 2:1-13 today, marking references to *harlotry* and *I will* as you did yesterday. Now, from what you've seen in chapters 1 and 2 so far, does this section refer to Hosea's wife, Gomer, or to the nation of Israel? Explain your answer.

Who are her lovers?   *The Lord is talking about Isreal.*

DAY FOUR

Today, read Hosea 2:14-23, marking references to *harlot* or *harlotry* and *I will* as you have before. Also mark *covenant* in red with a yellow outline. This word is key throughout the Bible.   *To bring God's People back*

Read Hosea 2 through and identify the shift that occurs in verse 14. How does this relate to the shift in Hosea 1:10?

Read through 2:14-23 again, marking the phrase *in that day*—a reference to the day of the Lord.   *Forgiveness, mercy*

DAY FIVE

Read Hosea 2:14-23 again, this time marking *compassion.*[2] Now go back and read Hosea 1 and 2 and mark *compassion.* When you come to the phrase *no compassion,* put a backward slash through the word, like this: compassion.

Who is the "her" in Hosea 2:14-20? What is the flow of thought in this chapter?   *Isreal (God's People)*

To make Things As They were before, to bring The People back to God

Compare 1 Peter 2:10 with Romans 9:22-26. Are God's messages in Hosea 1 and 2 consistent? What additional information do we learn with time? *This Mercy was*

Determine the theme of Hosea 2 and record it on HOSEA AT A GLANCE on page 61. *Not for The Jews only*

DAY SIX

Finally this week, read Hosea 3, marking *harlot*[3] as before. Also mark *love, return,* and time phrases. Mark *love* with a red heart and shade it red. Shade *return* yellow with a red arrow like this: *return.*

Now, how does the Lord's word to Hosea in this chapter parallel what He said in Hosea 1?

Looking at the time phrases in Hosea 3, in what order do the events occur? When does life seem dark for the sons of Israel in Hosea 3, and what is the message of hope in this chapter?

Determine the theme of Hosea 3 and record it on HOSEA AT A GLANCE on page 61.

DAY SEVEN

 Store in your heart: Hosea 2:23b

Read and discuss: Hosea 1:2-11; 2:14-23; 3:3-5; Romans 9:22-26

QUESTIONS FOR DISCUSSION OR INDIVIDUAL STUDY

- What significant meanings do Gomer's children's names have? *Besides being awful, They are Expressions of God*

- Who committed harlotry? What is the metaphorical meaning of *harlotry*? *Isreal*
  • To part from God, for other Gods

- Discuss the darkness Israel and Judah will live in because of their harlotry. *They will not have Gods Protecti or mercy, or anything*

- List the practical expressions of hope in Hosea 1–3. *God keeps his Promises, Gods mercy + forgivness*

- When will God provide this hope? What order do the events seem to happen in? *when David is King*

- What idols might you have in your life? Discuss what God might consider "harlotry" today.

- When you consider the darkness in and around you, what hope do you find in Hosea 1–3?

- How do these events show God's character? What traits do they show?

THOUGHT FOR THE WEEK

Sometimes life goes along just great, and then seemingly out of nowhere, calamity strikes. We don't always see clearly when things go well because we don't think we're doing anything wrong. At least that's how it seems in my life. I go on day to day, not really examining myself, and suddenly—*wham!*—I'm blindsided by something that produces darkness, something that tests me.

Not long ago, I had the opportunity to watch a partial eclipse of the sun. The moon was moving between the sun and the earth, blocking out some of the rays of the sun. I didn't know this was coming, and I wasn't paying attention. I was just leaving a hotel in Thessaloniki, Greece, when the doorman stopped me, pointed to the sun, and handed me some darkened glass. Even though the moon was partially blocking the sun, I couldn't watch the eclipse without this specially prepared glass.

God works this way too. He "dwells in unapproachable light, whom no man…can see" (1 Timothy 6:16), but through His Word "we see through a glass, darkly" until the day Jesus returns, when we'll be able to see Him face-to-face (1 Corinthians 13:12; 2 Corinthians 3:18 KJV). God hands us specially prepared glass for us to look through so we *can* see Him—so we can know His mind and will. (It's called the Bible!) He enables us to see both His marvelous light and the darkness that separates us from Him, darkness that blocks out the light, darkness He calls us out of (1 Peter 2:9).

The Word of God—written by holy men and translated and printed so we can observe, interpret, and apply it— reveals to us what light and darkness are. With this specially prepared glass, we can see when darkness blocks out light, but God first has to draw our attention to look through it.

God uses a variety of means to get our very distracted attention. Sometimes He uses natural disasters like hurricanes, floods, or fires. At other times He uses man-made catastrophes like automobile accidents, violent crimes, or war. When dark times like these come, we're alerted to look for help. We need someone, something, to give us hope. We reach out, searching for explanations—why we are where we are, why we experience difficult circumstances, why calamities happen, why pain and loss are parts of life.

God did something very different in Hosea's days to draw Israel's attention. His people needed someone to point out that their darkness was blocking out His light, and they needed a special lens to see it. To point out Israel's darkness, He commanded Hosea to marry a harlot and produce children of harlotry.

Normal education and experience tell us that eclipses are temporary phenomena—light doesn't disappear permanently. But someone who had never heard of an eclipse might be afraid that the sun was disappearing forever.

Similarly, without the Word of God, the deep darkness of catastrophes can easily cause people to think the sun won't shine again. People like this live without hope in the world.

But the Word of God tells us that God has a plan for us: to *give* us hope, show us compassion, and extend to us an opportunity to turn *from* our ways and *to* Him and His goodness. We find hope in God's character, which is revealed in His Word.

Where do we find hope in times of trouble, when life seems dark? In God's Word.

A LACK OF KNOWLEDGE

What happens when there's no knowledge of God in the land? What are the characteristics of a godless society? What's the language like? The thoughts and choices? The behaviors? How would these change if a society wholly adopted God's values?

DAY ONE

Read Hosea 4 today, marking *harlot* or *harlotry*[4] and *I will* as you did last week. Remember, if you add these words and their respective markings to a bookmark, you'll have an easy to use memory and reference tool.

Read Hosea 4 again, marking geographical references by double underlining them in green. Also mark *knowledge*.

DAY TWO

List what you learned from marking *knowledge*. Be sure your observations answer the who, what, when, where, why, and how questions. Here are a few sample questions you can use to interrogate the text: What's the status of knowledge in the land? What's happening to the people? What have they done?

Read through Hosea 4 again and underline references to *priest, people,* and *prophets.* Then list what each group is doing and what will happen to them.

DAY THREE

List what you learn about harlotry. Who is "playing the harlot"? How are they doing it? *Keep Knowledge*

Seek the Law *is a* *messenger*

From marking geographical references, where might Israel go, claiming allegiance to God? Read Malachi 2:7-9 and write down the responsibilities of priests. Then read Isaiah 28:7 and Jeremiah 5:30-31; 23:11-12. Is Israel's behavior in Hosea's time unique? *NO*

To sum up the chapter, what behaviors were common to the inhabitants of the land and why? *To turn from God*
not keep all His laws!

Finally, determine the theme of Hosea 4 and record it on HOSEA AT A GLANCE on page 61. *To have strong drink*

DAY FOUR

Read Hosea 5 today and mark *harlot* or *harlotry*[5] and *I will.* List what you learn from marking this key word and phrase.

When the kingdom divided in 931 BC, ten tribes including Ephraim formed the northern kingdom, which was called Israel. By 733 BC, Assyria had carried away all of these tribes except Ephraim and the part of Manasseh west of the Jordan River and north of Ephraim. So by Hosea's time, the northern kingdom was identified with Ephraim alone.

Read Hosea 5 again, this time marking every reference to *Ephraim* (you can use a star of David and/or the color blue—both appear in the flag of modern-day Israel).

DAY FIVE

From what you learned by marking *Ephraim*, list what Israel (or Ephraim) has done. Also list what God says He will do to them. *Both turned from God*
Ephraim — Committed Whoredom,

Isreal = Defiled

DAY SIX

Read Hosea 5:8 and 9:9 and then note what you learn about Gibeah. Then read Judges 19:13-30. Why did a trumpet have to be blown in Gibeah? What is God saying? Read Hosea 5:4; John 8:34-36; and Romans 6:6-18. What parallels do you see? What is the solution? How are slaves to sin freed? *By serving Righteousness,*
By Just Obeying The Lord this Laws or truths

Don't forget to determine the theme of Hosea 5 and record it on HOSEA AT A GLANCE on page 61.

DAY SEVEN

Store in your heart: Hosea 4:6a

Read and discuss: Hosea 4–5; Malachi 2:7-9; Romans 6:6-18

QUESTIONS FOR DISCUSSION OR INDIVIDUAL STUDY

- Discuss the thinking, choices, and behavior of those who have no knowledge of God.

- What consequences of rejecting knowledge has God revealed?

- What did Israel substitute for God?

- What do people today substitute for God? Where do they go for knowledge, advice, and direction?

- How are we freed from slavery to sin?

- Who can heal us from sin, and who can't?

THOUGHT FOR THE WEEK

Slavery is an ugly thing. Unfortunately the history of the United States was tarnished by European colonists who enslaved Africans, forcing them into wealth-creating, life-destroying labor. Many Americans are proud of their ancestors for not participating in this heinous act that continued for so long.

Today, slavery like this exists in local spots around the world. But Hosea's message to Ephraim countered a different kind of slavery, one that plagues everybody everywhere throughout history—slavery to sin.

Apart from the freedom only God can provide through His Son Jesus, mankind is enslaved to sin. Of course, people make many religious and secular claims to freedom. Hitler claimed that his work camps would make man free. In reality, they killed people. Financial security provides another popular claim to freedom. When you're financially secure, you're free to do anything you want.

But these are false ideas of freedom because they're based on false ideas of slavery.

Adam enslaved the human race to sin. By one man sin entered the world, and death through sin. All mankind from Adam forward is enslaved to sin and its payment, death. We can't escape from *this* slavery on our own, and by nature we don't want to. Instead, we redefine the problem so we can redefine the solution—invent our own ways to free ourselves. We think we can make something, buy something, or invent something to help us. We think we can either ignore sin (and its consequences) or flee it. Some people choose to believe there's no such thing as sin. If sin doesn't exist, then consequences don't exist either—judgments and penalties disappear with the bad behavior.

But even if a few individuals seem for a while to be able to get away with ignoring these things, the vast majority of people incorporated into societies are plagued by the nagging notion that deception, murder, and stealing are just plain wrong. They make laws that deal out punishment for such wrongs. Wrong *is* sin, and so sin exists. And people must somehow be enslaved by this sin, or crimes like these wouldn't have continued for thousands of years.

God spelled out precisely what sin is. He gave the Law to His people, Israel, at Mt. Sinai to show them what holiness and unholiness are. Paul tells us that God intended the Law to be a tutor to lead people to Christ. But Israel looked for another freedom—not a freedom *in* God but a freedom *from* God. They wanted out from under His rule.

God kept sending Israel prophets to tell them this was impossible, but Israel didn't listen. They didn't obey His commandments or worship Him the way He prescribed. They went their own way and worshiped other gods. So God sent prophets like Hosea to tell Israel they were sinning and what the consequences would be if they didn't stop.

God did the same for you and me. He sent His Son, Jesus, to declare the truth about the one and only way to become free from sin—through faith in the atoning sacrifice of Christ's death on the cross, which alone cleanses from sin and pays its penalty (death).

Freedom from slavery to sin, from bondage to the fear of death, from the dominion of Satan who has the power of death, is achieved by faith in the gospel. The Son of Man sets us free. We don't have to be destroyed for lack of knowledge. We don't have to reject the knowledge God has revealed. Jesus is able to heal us, to cure us from the wound that leads to death. Regardless of the sins we're guilty of, we have hope in Jesus Christ.

TRUSTING THE LORD

When you've strayed away from someone you once loved for no fault of theirs, how do you return? Isn't it hard? It means admitting that you have to change. And it means being forgiven. Are you ready to be forgiven? And *can* you be forgiven if you have strayed from God? With God, the answer is always "Yes, you're forgiven. Come back!"

DAY ONE

Read Hosea 6 today, marking *harlotry*[6] and *knowledge*[7] as before. Then read the chapter again and mark *return* and *covenant*. Remember, God operates on the basis of covenant, so we should always mark this key word.

DAY TWO

Read Hosea 6 and mark *Ephraim*. Then list what you learn about Ephraim's spiritual and moral deterioration, what judgments will follow, and any hope beyond judgment.

DAY THREE

How does Hosea 6:1-3 relate to Hosea 5?

Read 1 Samuel 7:3-4; Isaiah 55:7; Lamentations 3:40; and Joel 2:12-13. What is a "return to the Lord"?

Mark *loyalty*[8] in Hosea 6. The Hebrew word translated "loyalty" in Hosea 6 refers to lovingkindness, a covenant term. Read Micah 6:6-8 and Matthew 9:10-13, which quotes Hosea 6:6 but uses the word "compassion"[9] rather than "loyalty." What does God say about loyalty? Is this loyalty in your life?

Figure out a theme for Hosea 6 and record it on HOSEA AT A GLANCE on page 61.

DAY FOUR

Read Hosea 7, marking *Me* and *My* when they refer to God. Then list what you learn. What is Israel's problem?

Read the chapter again, marking *like*.[10] This word often introduces a simile (a figure of speech that draws a comparison). God uses these to point out Israel's sin and the consequences. List these comparisons.

DAY FIVE

Read Numbers 32:23; Job 34:21-22; Psalm 10:4,11; Isaiah 29:15-16; Jeremiah 23:23-24; and Ezekiel 8:12. Can we be engulfed in sin without God knowing about it?

DAY SIX

Read Hosea 7:13-16 again and mark the word *woe*. List reasons woe is coming upon Ephraim.

Where do you turn in calamity? Does the way you live, react, and respond reflect truth or lies about God?

Determine a theme for Hosea 7 and record it on HOSEA AT A GLANCE on page 61.

DAY SEVEN

 Store in your heart: Hosea 6:3

Read and discuss: Numbers 32:23; Jeremiah 23:23-24; Hosea 6–7

QUESTIONS FOR DISCUSSION OR INDIVIDUAL STUDY

- ∾ What does "return to the Lord" mean? How do we do this?

- ∾ What has Israel done that they need to return to the Lord?

- ∾ Discuss the possibility of hiding sin from God.

- ∾ Discuss loyalty to the Lord—Israel's and yours.

- ∾ What consequences will Israel face for their sin?

- ∾ Discuss the similes in Hosea 7 and how we can apply them to our lives today.

- ∾ What hope does God hold out in Hosea 6?

~ Discuss the relationship between the healing God plans to do for Israel and the healing He has done and will do for us.

~ How should we respond to God for what He has done for us?

THOUGHT FOR THE WEEK

"Let us press on to know the LORD" (Hosea 6:3). Paul exemplified this attitude in Philippians 3:12-14:

> Not that I have already obtained it or have already become perfect, but I press on so that I may lay hold of that for which also I was laid hold of by Christ Jesus. Brethren, I do not regard myself as having laid hold of it yet; but one thing I do: forgetting what lies behind and reaching forward to what lies ahead, I press on toward the goal for the prize of the upward call of God in Christ Jesus.

What an attitude to have! Do we live that way? Do we really forget what lies behind and reach forward, pressing on? So often we get caught up in the past, beating ourselves up, replaying our mistakes over and over. Our minds seem to be stuck on a nonstop "instant replay" of our shortcomings.

Is this what God wants us to do? He knows our mistakes. He knows our weaknesses. But He extends the prize just *beyond* reach so we will stretch for it, accomplishing much more for His glory than if it were within *easy* reach.

Scripture shows us that we can't be content with who we are, where we are, and what we've done. If we want to glorify God in our lives, we must, like Paul, press on. We can never know God intimately, experience Him fully, and taste His goodness completely unless we abandon self and run after Him.

We must be sure He has our best interests at heart and will bandage our injuries, heal our wounds, revive us, and raise us up from whatever pit we're in. The challenges in our lives that leave us feeling downtrodden, unappreciated, stressed out, depressed, or hopeless are not more than God can handle. He can and will come to us like the rain that waters the earth.

This is the truth we must believe to have and maintain hope. We must have confidence in the ultimate victory of life over death—in the triumph of Christ over all the rulers, authorities, and powers of this age and in our triumph and reign with Him. Otherwise, we will be defeated in attitude and heart, in spirit and mind. We won't operate in truth but in lies our adversary feeds us—such as *it's just too hard,* and *no one cares anyway.*

Hope replaces despair by the uplifting power of Jesus Christ and the purposeful decisions we make to place our trust and hope in the One who raises us up. We must know who He is, what He has done, and what our relationship to Him is to have confidence that He has our best interests at heart.

Stop now and read Philippians 3. Then ask yourself this simple question: *Do I have the confidence Paul had?* If not, why not? What's stopping you? That mind-set will make all the difference in your life.

THE DISCIPLINE
OF THE LORD

&n&n&n&n

When we do something wrong, when we sin against God or hurt someone, do we always experience consequences? Even if we're sorry, do we still need to undergo discipline? What purpose(s) do consequences serve? How can we reconcile God's attribute of love with harsh consequences? We can find answers to these questions in Hosea 8 and 9. God is holy and just.

DAY ONE

Add *idols* to your bookmark and then read Hosea 8, marking every reference to *idols* such as *calf, altars,* and *high places,* which you will see later, and every reference to *the nations.*[11] We usually mark *the nations* by shading in green and underlining in brown, but you can choose your own marking.

Read the chapter again, looking for a familiar maxim or saying. Now you know the context!

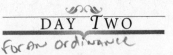

DAY TWO

For an ordinance

Read Numbers 10:8-10 and Ezekiel 33:1-11 today and compare them to Hosea 8:1. Why did God call for the trumpet to be blown? *(for awareness)*

Omri, the king of Israel, built the capital city of Samaria sometime around 880 BC, 125 years before Hosea's ministry. Eventually the entire region of Ephraim and Manasseh was named after this city, even to the time of Jesus. So here in Hosea 8, "Samaria" means Ephraim or Israel. Read Hosea 8 again and list or underline what Ephraim did that required the blowing of the trumpet.

DAY THREE

Read Hosea 8 one last time, this time marking *I will* as before and then listing in your notebook what God said He would do.

Hosea 8:7 is the maxim we hope you identified. Read Proverbs 22:8; Hosea 10:10; and Galatians 6:7-9. What insights do you find? *You reap what you sow*

Record a theme for Hosea 8 on HOSEA AT A GLANCE on page 61.

DAY FOUR

Read Hosea 9, marking key words on your bookmark. As you observe Hosea 9, especially mark geographical locations, including *Egypt* and *Assyria*.

DAY FIVE

Review Hosea 4:15. What did God say about Israel and Gilgal according to Hosea 9?

Read Joshua 4:19-24; 5:8-11; and 1 Samuel 11:14-15. Now compare with Amos 4:4 and 5:4-5. What do you glean from these passages?

DAY SIX

What do you learn from marking *Egypt* and *Assyria* in Hosea 9? Read 2 Kings 17:1-6,22-23 and then refer to the chart THE RULERS AND PROPHETS OF HOSEA'S TIME. How do these passages correlate with Deuteronomy 28:58-68?

Determine a theme for Hosea 9 and record it on HOSEA AT A GLANCE on page 61.

DAY SEVEN

 Store in your heart: Hosea 8:7

Read and discuss: Hosea 8:1-7; Ezekiel 33:1-11; Hosea 9:1-9

QUESTIONS FOR DISCUSSION OR INDIVIDUAL STUDY

∾ What do *sow the wind* and *reap the whirlwind* mean?

∾ Discuss the blowing of trumpets and the watchman on the wall.

∾ What role did Assyria play in Israel's history?

∾ What were God's commands about Egypt, and why did Hosea say the people would return to Egypt? What was his point?

∾ How do these chapters continue the theme of Israel's harlotry?

∾ Why does God proclaim all this judgment? Is He being fair?

∾ Discuss applications of these principles to your own lives. Be as specific as you can.

THOUGHT FOR THE WEEK

God made a covenant, and Israel entered into it. He took Israel to be His wife, but she quickly played the harlot with other gods, transgressing the covenant and rebelling against God's holy Law. The people built idols (golden calves), and God promised that they would reap what they sowed. They would be removed from the land He gave them and scattered among nations. They dove headfirst into depravity, and He would judge them for it.

But He had another purpose (beyond judgment)—to give Israel's southern sister, Judah, a warning and example. Not all the tribes of Israel lived in the northern kingdom. Benjamin and Judah made up the southern kingdom (Judah). Some Levites and other individuals from the ten tribes who remained faithful to the Lord lived in the southern kingdom too. If they would learn from Israel's faithlessness and judgment and heed the warning given to them, they would not have to bear the same consequences.

How does this apply to us? Hebrews 12:5-11 provides an explanation:

> And you have forgotten the exhortation which is addressed to you as sons,
>
> "MY SON, DO NOT REGARD LIGHTLY THE DISCIPLINE OF THE LORD,
>
> NOR FAINT WHEN YOU ARE REPROVED BY HIM;
>
> FOR THOSE WHOM THE LORD LOVES HE DISCIPLINES,
>
> AND HE SCOURGES EVERY SON WHOM HE RECEIVES."
>
> It is for discipline that you endure; God deals with you as with sons; for what son is there whom his father does not discipline? But if you are without discipline, of which all have become partakers, then you are illegitimate children and not sons. Furthermore, we had earthly fathers to discipline us, and we respected them; shall we not much rather be subject to the Father of spirits, and live? For they disciplined us for a short time as seemed best to them, but He disciplines us for our good, so that we may share His holiness. All discipline for the moment seems not to be joyful, but sorrowful; yet to those who have been trained by it, afterwards it yields the peaceful fruit of righteousness.

How quickly we remind ourselves that we're God's daughters and sons, fellow heirs with Christ of all the promises God made to His Son and adopted children. But we forget that as daughters and sons we also bear responsibility for obedience and right behavior before our holy Father in heaven.

We're also quick to remember that God is love. But we sometimes conveniently forget that love includes discipline. We must remember that God wants us to be holy, pure, blameless, and without spot or blemish at the coming of His Son from heaven. These things don't come easily—God offers no armchair, recliner, or hammock sanctifications. We are in a race to the finish line.

We focus on things that are uplifting, encouraging, and comforting, but we forget that God will give us exactly what we need to conform us to the image of His perfectly obedient, sinless Son. We won't obtain that perfection in this life, but because God the Father wants us to be spotless and blameless before His Son at His coming, He corrects us along the way.

2 Timothy 3:16-17 tells us that all of God's Word is profitable for correction:

> All Scripture is inspired by God and profitable for teaching, for reproof, for correction, for training in righteousness; so that the man of God may be adequate, equipped for every good work.

So Hosea 8 and 9 are profitable for teaching, reproof, correction, and training in righteousness. Hosea 8 and 9 make us adequate, equipped for every good work God has called us to, particularly to declare that Jesus is the way, the truth, and the life—that all who come to the Father come only through Him.

IS THERE ANY HOPE?

God threatens and threatens and threatens Israel with judgment—bad consequences for their sins. At the same time, He extends hope to them. Because of His righteousness and holiness, He can judge us and hold us accountable, but because of His grace, He is patient and willing to forgive. So long as Israel is alive, He gives them time to repent (Revelation 2:21) and offers hope before, during, and beyond the temporal judgments in this life.

DAY ONE

Read Hosea 10 today and mark key words from your bookmark. Find references to *idols, I will,* and geographical references. If other words and phrases seem key, be sure to mark them too.

Watch for similes (comparisons that start with *like* or *as*) and metaphors (comparisons without these words).

DAY TWO

How is Israel's heart faithless? Read Hosea 2:13; 8:14; and 13:6. Then read Deuteronomy 8:11-14,19 and 32:16-18.

What can we learn from Israel's sins? Read Deuteronomy 4:9-10; Psalm 103:2-5; 119:92-93; and Hosea 8:12.

DAY THREE

Hosea has revealed a pattern of idolatry. Did it start there? Read Exodus 32:1-10.

Note what these prophets say about idols: David (Psalm 115:1-8), Isaiah (44:9-20), and Ezekiel (14:2-6).

What about today—New Testament times? Read Romans 1:21-24; 1 Corinthians 8:4-6; 10:19-21; and Ephesians 5:5-10. What do you conclude?

Determine a theme for Hosea 10 and record it on HOSEA AT A GLANCE on page 61.

DAY FOUR

Read Hosea 11 and mark the following key words from your bookmark: *I will, idols, love,*[12] *turn, return.*[13] Also mark geographical references. If *turn* and *return* are used negatively, draw slashes through them. Also identify similes and metaphors.

DAY FIVE

List what you learn about the state of the people and the consequences of their sin from Hosea 11:1-7.

Now list some elements of hope according to Hosea 11:8-12.

Assyria will rule them
No understanding of God
They will be to war or

He will not let the Totally go.
He will not destroy Them

DAY SIX

Admah and Zeboiim are cities near Sodom and Gomorrah. Read Genesis 10:15-19; 14:1-9 and Deuteronomy 29:22-29. What does God say He *doesn't* want to do to Israel in Hosea 11:8-9?

Read Ezekiel 36:24-28. When life seems dark for Israel, where is their hope?

Finally, determine the theme of Hosea 11 and record it on HOSEA AT A GLANCE on page 61.

DAY SEVEN

Store in your heart: Hosea 11:1

Read and discuss: Hosea 10:1-4,11-15; 11:1-4,8-11; Romans 1:21-24

QUESTIONS FOR DISCUSSION OR INDIVIDUAL STUDY

∾ Describe the sins and the sinful lifestyle of Israel.

∾   What metaphors and similes in these chapters help you understand God's relationship to Israel?

∾   What insights about Israel's sins can we apply to our lives today?

∾   How did God care for Israel?

∾   What was Israel's response to God's love?

∾   Why should we hope in God?

THOUGHT FOR THE WEEK

Someone has said that if you can convince a man there's no hope, he will curse the day he was born. Hope is an indispensable quality of life.

Years ago a Navy S-4 submarine was rammed by another ship and quickly sank, trapping its entire crew. Ships rushed to the scene off the coast of Massachusetts. A diver placed his helmeted ear to the side of the vessel and listened. Someone was tapping out a question using the dots and dashes of Morse code. The question came slowly: "Is…there…any…hope?"

This seems to be the cry of humanity: "Is there any hope?" The answer is Yes there is! Hope is one of the many qualities of life in Christ![1]

This scenario reminds me of the days when Israel heard the word of the Lord through Hosea. They were told they were trapped, doomed, heading for destruction. Yet God mingled words of hope with words of judgment. Despite the

---

1. P.L. Tan, *Encyclopedia of 7700 Illustrations* (Garland, TX: Bible Communications, 1996).

warning of punishment for all their sins, God held out hope. He seems to have built into all men this need to find hope in the darkest hour. This makes us unique creatures. We have a *fallen* ability to despair but the *created* ability to hope—to believe in God's salvation.

In the Bible, hope is quite different from the hope the men in the submarine had. Their hope was subjective—wishful thinking; they weren't sure they had any objective hope. And even if there had been some element of objectivity, like the sounds of someone coming to rescue them, it would come with no guarantees. Rescue would still be uncertain, a probability at best, not a fact. This is the best man has to offer.

Hope in God is radically different. It's certainty of God's character and promises. Hope in God's grace is as certain as knowledge of His judgment. They are two sides of the same coin. Because God is holy and just, He must judge sin. But He has done this in His Son, whom "He made...to be sin on our behalf" (2 Corinthians 5:21). Do you see how our faith in God's holiness and judgment is actually our faith in God's grace—two sides of one faith coin?

God's mercy toward sinners is sure. He bore our sins so we would not have to. He made a way for us to live when we deserved to die. Our hope for our personal futures, our sanctification and glorification, is based on nothing less than the character of God, which is fully expressed in Jesus.

A rock-solid foundation. Let's never lose hope, therefore, but always be ready to give an account for the hope that is within us:

> But sanctify Christ as Lord in your hearts, always being ready to make a defense to everyone who asks you to give an account for the hope that is in you, yet with gentleness and reverence (1 Peter 3:15).

GOD'S SOLUTIONS
TO OUR PROBLEMS

When we try to find our own solutions to our problems, we miss God. He has shown us over and over in Scripture that He leads, provides, and gives examples to teach us. But we still turn to other people, places, and things for answers. God has a different opinion. *He* thinks we should turn to *Him*.

DAY ONE

Read Hosea 12, marking the key words and phrases on your bookmark. Especially note *covenant*[14] and *prophet*.

DAY TWO

Look back at every place you marked *covenant* in Hosea (2:18; 6:7; 8:1; 10:4). Whom was Israel supposed to be in covenant with? What had Israel done?

Let's look at Israel's relationship with Assyria and Egypt in Hosea. Read Hosea 5:13; 7:11; 8:9,13; 9:3; and 11:5. Record your insights.

Whom should Ephraim have put their trust in?

DAY THREE

We don't want you to miss the significance of references to *Jacob*, so read through Hosea 12:2-6 again and mark this name.

Now read Genesis 25:21-26; 32:22-32; 35:1-7,9-15 to familiarize yourself with the stories referenced in Hosea 12:2-6. What point is God making with Ephraim through the account of Jacob? From what you've seen in Hosea, what is Ephraim supposed to do?

DAY FOUR

Read Hosea 12:5 again. Translations vary, but compare Exodus 3:14-15 to Hosea 12:5. Whichever translation you use, you should be able to catch the significance.

Now read Hosea 12:6 again. What does God call Ephraim to do and why?

DAY FIVE

Now read Hosea 12:7-8 again. What do you think God is saying about Ephraim?

It can be easier to grasp many of Hosea's allusions by reading a few select verses elsewhere in the Old Testament, letting Scripture interpret Scripture. Read Hosea 12:9; Leviticus 23:39-43; and Zechariah 14:16-19.

Read Hosea 12:13 and then Deuteronomy 34:10. What did you learn from marking *prophets* in this chapter? How significant were they to Israel?

DAY SIX

Read Hosea 12:12-14 and record what you learn about Jacob's life before his name was changed to Israel.

What point do you think Hosea was trying to make in verses 12-13? Read Genesis 28:1-2; 29:20-30; and Exodus 13:3. Think about what God has done for Israel.

Determine a theme for Hosea 12 and then record it on HOSEA AT A GLANCE on page 61.

DAY SEVEN

 Store in your heart: Hosea 12:6

Read and discuss: Hosea 12; Genesis 25:21-26; 32:22-32; 35:1-7,9-15

QUESTIONS FOR DISCUSSION OR INDIVIDUAL STUDY

∾ Discuss Jacob's life—his birth, marriage, and relationship to Esau.

∾ Now relate Jacob's life to Hosea 12. What lessons should we learn?

∾ Discuss Ephraim's reliance on Assyria and Egypt. What can we apply to our lives?

∾ What value does God place on the prophets He sent to Israel? How should we view the prophetic Word, Scripture?

∾ Have you ever wrestled with God? What is God saying to you in this lesson?

THOUGHT FOR THE WEEK

Jacob wrestled with God. Wrestling is an activity in which each opponent tries to gain advantage over the other with holds, maneuvers, leverage, strength...even deception. Now think about everything involved in this statement: "He [Jacob] contended with God. Yes, he wrestled with the angel" (Hosea 12:4).

Jacob clearly didn't know he was wrestling with God at the beginning, but in the end he did. He suffered a dislocated hip in the struggle. He didn't win, but he did suffer from the struggle.

What happens to us when we wrestle with issues—when we grapple, struggle, maneuver, apply leverage, and so on? When a problem comes up and we seek a solution, do we dive right in, applying skills we've learned and practiced?

If we're going to apply *all* our skills, we will necessarily include the skill of seeking God. In the struggle to find a solution, we can choose from two paths—seek God or search without God, seek His solution or someone else's (including our own). How easily we miss this critical distinction.

This is a stunning revelation to "fixers." We see a problem and jump right in to fix it. We give advice; we do things to help; we enter the fray because we *know* how to fix. We've got experience, education, life skills. We're experts...professionals. Take it from us!

How often when faced with a problem do we stop to take a breath and ask God for wisdom? Do we ever even ask God whether we should enter a fray at all? The most common dilemma is whether we should offer a solution or let people struggle through a problem themselves.

Too often, I think, we rob people of the benefit of struggling to find God's solution. If we offer our help too quickly, the faith-building, character-strengthening aspects of struggle are bypassed. How will we grow in faith, how will our character be strengthened, if others give us solutions? If we never get to work through issues, seeking God's wisdom and strength, how will we ever learn to depend on Him rather than our neighbor, friend, or family?

Radical thought, isn't it? We want to help. We don't want those we love to suffer and struggle. But struggles strengthen. Baby birds peck their way through shells to gain the strength they need to survive. When we break open the shell for them, they usually die early.

So it is with us. When we peck our way through our problems, we are strengthened. If we do things God's intended way—turn directly to Him in prayer, seek His revealed will through His Word, and obey it—we are strengthened.

If we let others fix our problems, we may learn one more skill to use when the problem arises again, but we won't be ready for any new challenges.

Wrestling our way through problems while seeking God's wisdom builds problem-solving skills that will equip us for all of life's challenges. We learn how to seek God, not fix problems. We don't run to Assyria or Egypt; we turn to God and wait for Him continually.

How Do I Get Rid of My Guilt?

When you've sinned, who takes away the guilt? Who will take away your iniquity and receive you graciously, regardless of how grievous the sin? Who provides such things for you? The Lord your God!

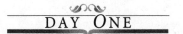

DAY ONE

Read Hosea 13 today, marking the key words you've listed on your bookmark. Include geographical references, metaphors, and similes.

According to Hosea 13:1-2, what was the people's downfall? Read 1 Kings 12:25-33 and 16:29-33.

DAY TWO

List what you learn about Ephraim from the similes in Hosea 13:3.

What has God done for the people according to Hosea 13:4-5? What's the first word of verse 4 and why is it significant?

How did Ephraim respond to God?

List what God says He'll do according to Ephraim's response. Why will He do this? Is this fair? Read Deuteronomy 6:13-15 before you answer.

DAY THREE

According to Hosea 13:9-10, who helps and who can't help?

Read 1 Samuel 8:4-8; 9:17 and 1 Chronicles 10:13-14. How do these explain Hosea 13:9-10?

What is going to happen to Ephraim according to Hosea 13:12-16?

Determine the theme of Hosea 13 and record it on HOSEA AT A GLANCE on page 61.

DAY FOUR

We've come to our final chapter of Hosea, just nine verses long. Before you mark anything, read it just to get the spirit or mood of the chapter. How does it differ from Hosea 13?

Now read Hosea 14 again and mark the key words and phrases from your bookmark. Don't miss *return*.

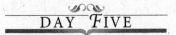

DAY FIVE

In this chapter, marking *God* is especially helpful. After you have done this, list what you learn about God, especially what He will do for Israel. What will He do, and what will He be like?

Look at the similes and metaphors about Israel. What will become of Israel?

What will be taken away from Israel? How does this relate to all you've seen in Hosea about Israel?

DAY SIX

Read Deuteronomy 4:27-31. How old is this message of redemption and compassion?

Read Isaiah 42:23–43:7 and 55:6-7. Was Hosea's message unique, or had God sent other prophets?

Let's look at a few last verses that will help us use Scripture to interpret Scripture. Read Acts 26:20; 1 John 1:9; and Revelation 2:5. Does God's message to Israel apply to you in any way?

Don't forget to determine the theme of Hosea 14 and record it on HOSEA AT A GLANCE on page 61.

DAY SEVEN

 Store in your heart: Hosea 14:9

Read and discuss: Isaiah 42:23–43:7; Hosea 13–14; Acts 26:20; 1 John 1:9

QUESTIONS FOR DISCUSSION OR INDIVIDUAL STUDY

- ∾ Discuss Israel's sin. What have they done to make God angry?

- ∾ What was God's response to their sin in Hosea 13? Did it change in Hosea 14?

- ∾ Did you see an *apparent* inconsistency in God's mind in these chapters? Discuss the relationship of compassion to justice. How would you reconcile them?

- ∾ What does God ask Israel to do once they've sinned? What does He ask you to do when you've sinned?

- ∾ How is God's response to Israel consistent with His promises in the New Testament?

- ∾ Throughout Hosea, what hope for the future do you see?

THOUGHT FOR THE WEEK

The title of this study booklet is *Finding Hope When Life Seems Dark*. For seven weeks we have pored over Hosea—14 chapters filled with descriptions of Israel's sins, God's righteous anger and judgment, and in the end, His extension of hope to the hopeless. He commands His people to return to Him, and He promises healing.

God tells Hosea to take a prostitute for his wife and have children with her—a picture of God's marriage to Israel. God knew from eternity that His bride would stray from

Him. He knew she would play the harlot with foreign gods, idols made with human hands, objects that are not really gods at all. He knew she would reject Him regardless of how many times He called, but He continued to call, always holding out the hope of redemption.

What's really amazing in these accounts of Israel's history is that God never gives up on His people. His anger burns only enough to turn them back to Him, never to destroy them completely.

So it is with us today. When we stray, God uses whatever means are necessary to draw us back because He has promised never to forsake us. He has placed us in the palm of His hand, and no one can pluck us out. Nothing can separate us from the love of God in Christ Jesus. We have hope because God promises us hope, and His promises are sure. Unlike man, God does not renege on promises. His Word is constant. He is constant—the same yesterday, today, and forever.

This is how we have hope. We have confidence in the sameness of God's character, as Hebrews 6:17-20 tells us:

> In the same way God, desiring even more to show to the heirs of the promise the unchangeableness of His purpose, interposed with an oath, so that by two unchangeable things in which it is impossible for God to lie, we who have taken refuge would have strong encouragement to take hold of the hope set before us. This hope we have as an anchor of the soul, a hope both sure and steadfast and one which enters within the veil, where Jesus has entered as a forerunner for us, having become a high priest forever according to the order of Melchizedek.

Life seems darkest when we see the reality of our sin. How dark it is in the light of God's holiness! At that moment, we're brought low by the rightness of God's judgment.

But we have hope because we have forgiveness. We know that Christ shed His blood for the forgiveness of our sins, and His righteousness is imputed to us by faith so that we can be clothed in it. God Himself does not see sin underneath His perfect Son's righteousness, which propitiates and satisfies God. This is our confidence to draw near to His throne of grace, to boldly approach Him through the mercy seat cleansed by Jesus' blood. And we know our consciences are cleansed by this same blood. Rejoice!

Theme of Hosea:

SEGMENT DIVISIONS

		CHAPTER THEMES
		1
		2
		3
		4
		5
		6
		7
		8
		9
		10
		11 The wrath of God
		12
		13
		14

Author:

Date:

Purpose:

Key Words:

harlot (harlotry)

I will

covenant

in that day

compassion

love

return

knowledge

Ephraim

idols

nations

prophets

MICAH

INTRODUCTION TO MICAH

Micah of Moresheth prophesied in the days of Hosea and Isaiah. But while Hosea prophesied to the northern kingdom, Israel, Micah (like Isaiah) prophesied to the southern kingdom, Judah. Yet he addressed his message to Samaria—another name for the northern kingdom. The captive kingdom was to be Judah's example. If Judah paid attention to what happened in Samaria, they could avoid the judgments Samaria brought on herself.

Would they heed the warning?

$\mathcal{H}$OW $\mathcal{I}$S $\mathcal{Y}$OUR $\mathcal{C}$OMMITMENT TO $\mathcal{T}$RUTH?

In the midst of darkness there is always light because *God is light.*

In the midst of despair there is always hope because *God is hope.*

In the midst of corruption and lies there is pure truth, the Word of the Lord, because *God is not silent.*

Who is like Jehovah?

DAY ONE

Read Micah 1:1 and identify the author, the timing of the message, and the basic content of the message.

Compare Hosea 1:1-2 and Isaiah 1:1 with Micah 1:1. Refer to the chart THE RULERS AND PROPHETS OF MICAH'S TIME on page 81 to see where Micah fits chronologically.

Now read Micah 1:2 and underline *hear* and *listen.* Be sure to list Micah's key words on a bookmark for easy reference.

Now read Micah 3:1 and 6:1. These phrases show us that Micah contains three oracles or messages. There are two instances of *hear this,* but the phrase *hear now* indicates the start of new messages.

Now read chapter 1 and mark all clear references to *Samaria* (the capital of Israel, the northern kingdom) one way and *Jerusalem* (the capital of Judah, the southern kingdom) another (not their pronouns and synonyms, just their names).

Who will receive this first message? What will happen to them? Why?

What key word from Hosea do you see in verse 7?

Samaria —
Jerusalem —

DAY TWO

Read Micah 1 again and mark *sin*[1] and *calamity* in addition to time phrases and geographical references.

What did Micah say he has to do?

What did you learn from marking *sin*?

What was the beginning of sin to Jerusalem?

Assyria began its process of enslaving the northern kingdom (Israel) in 733 BC, and by 722 BC all Samaria was captive. In 701 BC Assyria moved against Judah, besieging the city of Lachish (southwest of Jerusalem) and from there advancing to the gates of Jerusalem.

Sin begins and advances like this. Read James 1:13-15 and 1 Corinthians 15:33.

DAY THREE

Read 2 Samuel 5:7; 2 Kings 19:20-21,31; and Psalm 9:11-14. In the context of Micah 1, what is *the daughter of Zion* synonymous with?

Mark *daughter of Zion* accordingly.

Read Micah 1 again and mark references to *God.* What do you learn about God from this chapter? How can you apply this to your life?

Don't forget to determine the theme of Micah 1 and record it on MICAH AT A GLANCE on page 82.

DAY FOUR

Read Micah 2 and mark the key words you marked previously. Add the following: *evil,*[2] *iniquity, destruction*[3] *(destroy[ed]), woe, Spirit,* and *remnant.*

DAY FIVE

What do you learn from marking synonyms of *sin* in chapter 2? Who's sinning? What will happen to them? Who will do it?

Read Micah 2:6-11 and mark references to *speaking.* Record what you learn about the speakers.

What do you think about the latter part of Micah 2:7: "Do not My words do good to the one walking uprightly?" How can you apply this to your life?

DAY SIX

What did you learn from marking *God* in chapter 2? Does this make you feel threatened or comforted?

Read Micah 2:12-13 again and list what you learn from marking *remnant*.

Is the mood here different from the mood in the rest of Micah 1–2?

Determine a theme for Micah 2 and record it on MICAH AT A GLANCE on page 82.

DAY SEVEN

 Store in your heart: Micah 2:13
Read and discuss: Micah 1–2

QUESTIONS FOR DISCUSSION OR INDIVIDUAL STUDY

- ∞ Review the historical setting of Micah, including the timing of kings, prophets, and kingdoms.

- ∞ Discuss the effect Samaria's and Judah's sin had on the world.

- ∞ How did Samaria's sin affect Judah?

- ∞ What does Micah feel compelled to do because of this impact? Why?

- ∞ How would you apply Micah's action to your own life?

- ∞ How did God react to sin? Do you think He reacts differently today from the way He did in Micah's days?

- ∞ What hope do you see in Micah 2?

- ∞ What do you learn about God this week that challenges your thinking or that brings you comfort and hope?

THOUGHT FOR THE WEEK

Surely God judges sinners, and His judgments affect other people. The high places of the earth, the mountains, and the valleys all bore consequences from Jacob's (Israel's) rebellion.

How would you react to this message from the Lord? Would you be willing to go barefoot and naked, lament like jackals, and mourn like ostriches if *your* people were at fault? Or would you simply write them off as worthy of judgment and wait for the ax from heaven to fall? Do you think these very different reactions have any bearing on who gets judged and how harshly? Can prayer and fasting make a dent in a judgment or a difference in the size of a remnant?

More often we shake our heads and chat about how bad things are in our society, using words like *ungodly, un-Christian, immoral, wrong,* and *disrespectful.* But we need to do much more. We need first to declare that judgment is coming, and then, like the people of Nineveh in the days of Jonah (starting with its king, no less), we need to pray and fast with the hope that God will delay or some other way mitigate it, reducing its scope and severity with mercy (Ezra 9:13).

Have you ever thought about how committed to truth you are by *God's* measures? (Commitment includes not only *knowing* truth but also *obeying* and *declaring* it.) What would stir you up enough to be a Micah?

We can measure our commitment to truth by honestly assessing how much we love God, hate sin, and love our neighbor as ourselves. God hates sin. If we love God, we should hate sin the way He hates it. We should be as committed as He is to identifying sin and declaring its consequences. And if we love people the way He does, we should be willing to sacrifice to keep them from the destruction they will suffer if they don't repent. A mother is willing to sacrifice everything to rescue her child from a burning building because she knows how serious the situation is. We should be just as willing to sacrifice to help people avoid the burning consequences of their sin.

Maybe we *don't* love people and hate sin as much or as consistently as God does. But we can move past honest apathy. Prophets like Micah stir up our hearts, our feet, and our mouths to action. If we're going to help rescue our societies, we *must* become part of the outcry against sin, part of the warning of coming destruction...even if others mock us as fools and laugh at us to scorn.

We know the truth. Why don't we share it? Why are we intimidated by a world that calls us fools *when we know the opposite is true?* Why not rather follow Paul and boldly admit, "We are fools for Christ's sake" (1 Corinthians 4:10)? This is a *good* identity—an admission that everybody is a fool for one thing or another. Better to be a fool for truth than for a lie, for a living Christ than for a perishing world, for an eternal life with Him than for a short life of pleasure that ends in destruction.

The last two verses of Micah 2 motivate us to hope. God will keep and gather a remnant and shepherd these sheep. The "breaker" goes up before them, and they "break out," pass through the gate, and go out. Their King goes before them, and the Lord leads.

This is the good news! The Lord is coming again to shepherd His flock, going before them as King of kings and Lord of lords! This is a truth to declare...to tell the nations!

KNOWING THE PURPOSES OF GOD

> But they do not know the thoughts of the
> LORD, And they do not understand His pur-
> pose (Micah 4:12).

Think of what happens when we don't understand God's purpose. We miss opportunities to grow in faith. Our thoughts, decisions, and actions carry us in wrong directions—every which way but up!

What can we do to understand God and His purposes? Stay in His Word—that's where He reveals Himself, so that's where we can meet Him.

DAY ONE

Last week we underlined the phrase *hear now,* which indicates the start of oracles (messages) in the book. As you begin Micah 3, note that it introduces a new oracle.

Read Micah 3 and mark the key words on your bookmark. Add the words *prophets* and *temple*[4] and mark them too. Mark *Zion* the same way you mark *Jerusalem.*

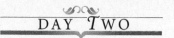

DAY TWO

List the groups of people God speaks about in Micah 3 and what you learn about them.

How do the prophets who lead the people astray compare with Micah, a true prophet of God?

Read 2 Peter 1:19–2:3 and answer the 5 W's and an H concerning the false and the true prophets and prophecies.

If you have time, read 2 Timothy 4:1-4 and compare it to 2 Peter 1:19–2:3.

Record a theme for Micah 3 on MICAH AT A GLANCE on page 82.

DAY THREE

Read Micah 4, marking the key words on your bookmark. Add *mountain* and *nations*.[5] Be sure to mark time references and geographical locations.

DAY FOUR

What did you learn from marking references to *Zion* in chapter 4?

Read chapter 4 again. What will happen in the last days?

Record a theme for Micah 4 on MICAH AT A GLANCE on page 82.

DAY FIVE

Read Micah 5, marking the key words from your bookmark.

DAY SIX

What do you learn about the person described in Micah 5:2-5?

Read Matthew 2:1,3-6 and Isaiah 9:6-7, and compare them to Micah 5:2.

What do you learn from marking *remnant* in Micah 5? Go back and read Micah 2:12 and 4:7, and compare them with Micah 5.

What will happen "in that day"?

Record your theme for Micah 5 on MICAH AT A GLANCE on page 82.

DAY SEVEN

 Store in your heart: Micah 5:2

Read and discuss: Micah 3:5-12; 4:1-8; 5:2-5,7-9; Matthew 2:1,3-6

QUESTIONS FOR DISCUSSION OR INDIVIDUAL STUDY

∽ Discuss those who led Israel astray and how they did it.

- ∾ What will happen because of them?

- ∾ What hope does Micah reveal for Israel? Discuss what will happen and when.

- ∾ Discuss the significance of the ruler from Bethlehem.

- ∾ What happens to the remnant? What is their relationship to the Lord?

- ∾ Discuss the events that will happen "in that day."

- ∾ How does a nation's failure to understand God's purpose affect its future?

THOUGHT FOR THE WEEK

Failure to understand God's dealings with Israel led nations to gloat over its misfortune. But they could see only the present. Because they didn't know the word of the Lord through Micah, they couldn't know Israel's future.

They couldn't know that even though God planned to bring Judah into captivity in Babylon, He would later rescue them from their enemies. He planned subjugation to reveal His sovereign justice but also redemption to reveal His patient mercy and love. The people had turned away from Him, so He was just in letting them suffer consequences. But He would later free them from their enemies to show the redemptive character of His love.

Through Micah God told Israel that prophets, priests, a temple, and Jerusalem's walls were not enough to protect them. They needed to live His way and trust Him. So He subjugated them, making them the tail and someone else the head.

Perhaps you don't relate to Israel. After all, Micah lived 2700 years ago, and you may feel that these people were very different from us and had a special relationship to God. But if you have believed the gospel, according to John 1:12 *you* have a special relationship to God; you are a child of God.

> But as many as received Him, to them He gave the right to become children of God, even to those who believe in His name.

God doesn't change—He's the same yesterday, today, and forever. His character *is* what it *was* in the days of Micah. He is still just, loving, all-knowing, and all-powerful. Because He's our Father, He disciplines us as children (Hebrews 12:4-11).

Understanding God's purposes is very important—and especially His reasons for disciplining us. We're not always obedient; we're not sinless in this life. We need to understand that life's difficulties are here to strengthen our faith. We won't always fully understand why some things happen to us. But we need to know that they aren't always *bad;* God has a higher purpose in mind. We need to look beyond the moment. Bad things are means, not ends.

When you understand God's ways, you can change your thinking in difficult times and begin to ask questions like *What do You want me to learn, Lord?* and *What should I change?* You may not need to change anything but the object of your trust—Him more, yourself less. All of us are self-reliant to some degree. We love to fix things and find solutions. We need to learn to depend on *God's* solutions.

God will someday put Israel in a position of safety and security. He will provide a Shepherd to care for them. In fact, He has already provided the Shepherd, who cares for His people (those who believe in Him) now. Our safety and security are guaranteed by Him through our faith, regardless of what happens to us in this life.

The challenge is to rest in this truth when things don't go well. We must believe God's truth and reject the lies the enemy uses to keep us from resting fully in God. When life seems dark, we find hope in God.

Make it your purpose to spend time with God in His Word to know Him intimately. Spend time with Him in prayer and worship. Draw near *to* Him and draw strength *from* Him. He will be your peace.

WHAT DELIGHTS THE LORD?

What a God we have! Who is like Jehovah? Do you understand, Beloved, that our God, Jehovah, does not retain His anger forever because He delights in unchanging love?

What a difference this truth can make in your relationship with Him!

DAY ONE

Chapter 6 starts a new oracle. How can you tell?

Read Micah 6 today, marking key words from your bookmark. Add *indictment*.[6]

DAY TWO

Answer the 5 W's and an H about the Lord's indictment. Read Leviticus 25:23; Deuteronomy 11:16-17; and 1 Kings 14:22-23. Whom does the land belong to? What was Israel not to do with the land? What have they done? Did they deserve indictment?

What does the Lord want instead of sacrifice? Read Micah 1–5 and briefly list the evidence that the people were not doing what He required. How does this tie into the indictment?

DAY THREE

Read Micah 6:9-16. List the sins Israel was guilty of and their consequences.

Are *any* sins worth their consequences?

Don't forget to determine the theme of Micah 6 and record it on MICAH AT A GLANCE on page 82.

DAY FOUR

Read Micah 7 and mark the words on your bookmark. Don't miss geographical locations, time references, and the key word *remnant*. Mark *Lord* and *love*.[7]

DAY FIVE

Who is speaking in Micah 7:1-10? What is he thinking? Is he justified?

What does he say he'll do? How does this differ from others around him?

What does Micah base his confidence in the Lord on? Judging from what you've seen elsewhere in Micah, is this confidence justified?

DAY SIX

What verse in chapter 7 marks a scenario shift to the future? Describe Micah's use of *that day*.

What will the Lord do then?

What did you learn from marking references to *the Lord*?

What verses in this chapter give you hope?

Now scan the entire book and list what you learn about the *remnant*.

Record a theme for Micah 7 on MICAH AT A GLANCE on page 82.

DAY SEVEN

Store in your heart: Micah 6:8

Read and discuss: Micah 6:1-8; 7:7-9,14-20

QUESTIONS FOR DISCUSSION OR INDIVIDUAL STUDY

ᴥ Discuss Micah's attitude toward the Lord.

ᴥ Do you relate to Micah? Why or why not?

ᴥ Discuss what you learned from Micah about the remnant.

   ∾ Discuss what you learned from Micah about the Lord.

   ∾ How might you apply these insights about the Lord to your life?

THOUGHT FOR THE WEEK

In Micah 6:8, God tells us what is good and what He requires. Do you live this way? Do you do justice, love kindness, and walk humbly before Him? These characteristics are commended in Ephesians, Colossians, Philippians, and other New Testament books. They define living in the Spirit.

First Samuel 15:22-23 records these words, which Samuel spoke to Saul:

> Has the Lord as much delight in burnt offerings
>   and sacrifices
> As in obeying the voice of the Lord?
> Behold, to obey is better than sacrifice,
> And to heed than the fat of rams.
> For rebellion is as the sin of divination,
> And insubordination is as iniquity and
>   idolatry.
> Because you have rejected the word of the
>   LORD,
> He has also rejected you from being king.

Under Saul, Israel made the mistake of thinking worship rituals please God. God ordained sacrifices, but what He has always wanted is obedience. Samuel likens rebellion to divination, and insubordination to iniquity and idolatry. We can act out a ritual and never truly worship God in our lives.

This was Israel's condition in Micah's day. They lived out the form of worship God gave them, but in their hearts they were rebels. God knows the heart. He judges the thoughts and intentions of the heart through His Word.

If we live the way Israel was living, we may fool people around us, but we won't fool God. He knows our thoughts. He sees right through us.

We're called to be living sacrifices, which means our self-ishness must be sacrificed—subjected (obedient) to His will. If we truly understand God's unchanging love and compassion, we can live before Him in righteousness and truth. We don't have to fear separation from Christ. We have hope in Him.

When things are dark, when things don't seem to be going right in our lives, we can trust that God loves us and will have compassion on us. Jesus will plead our case to His Father, and He will vindicate us, bring us into light, and show us His righteousness. He will shepherd us and give us peace and rest.

THE RULERS AND PROPHETS OF MICAH'S TIME

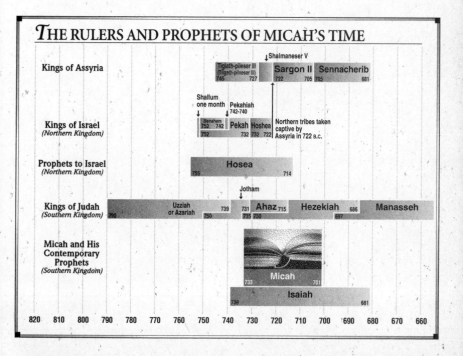

Theme of Micah:

Author:

Date:

Purpose:

Key Words:

Samaria

Jerusalem

Zion

destroy(ed)
(destruction)

remnant

in that day (in
the last days)

My (Your, His)
people

sin (iniquity,
evil)

SEGMENT DIVISIONS

		CHAPTER THEMES
		1
		2
		3
		4
		5
		6
		7

Nahum

INTRODUCTION TO NAHUM

ᘓᘓᘓᘓᘓ

More than a hundred years before Nahum ministered, Jonah preached to Nineveh, the capital city of Assyria. The people repented, and God spared them. But less than 50 years later, the Assyrians attacked Israel and took most of its tribes captive. By 722 BC, they had subjugated all the northern tribes. A few people remained, but Assyria replaced the captives with captives from other lands. Judah alone remained free. Assyria attacked Judah in the days of Hezekiah, but the Lord spared them. Fifty years later, the Lord sent Nahum with a message to Assyria.

You Can't Fool God

Can a nation forget God, act cruelly, and escape His judgments? And what does the answer mean to people living in the twenty-first century, like us?

DAY ONE

Read Nahum 1 and mark references (including pronouns) to *Nineveh*, *Judah*, and *God*. Be careful to mark *they* and *you* in verses 12-13 appropriately (that is, according to the subjects they refer to).

DAY TWO

Now list what you learned about *Nineveh*, *Judah*, and *God* in chapter 1.

Where is hope? Who is it for? List Judah's hopes.

Determine the theme of Nahum 1 and record it on NAHUM AT A GLANCE on page 90.

DAY THREE

Read Nahum 2, marking references to *Nineveh, Judah,* and *God* again. Watch for changes between *you* and *them* in Nahum 1:15 and 2:1-2—it's easy to confuse subjects, so go slowly! The messages of the chapters go together, so the context will help you.

DAY FOUR

What's Nineveh's destiny?

What hope does God hold out for Judah?

How do Nahum 1 and 2 fit together?

Don't forget to determine the theme of Nahum 2 and record it on NAHUM AT A GLANCE on page 90.

DAY FIVE

Read Nahum 3, marking references to *Nineveh, God, harlotry,*[1] and *the nations,* and double underlining all geographical references.

DAY SIX

As you've done before with other judgments, list what God says He will do to Nineveh. It may be good to consolidate your lists from all three chapters.

Why is God so judgmental?

Don't forget to determine the theme of Nahum 3 and record it on NAHUM AT A GLANCE on page 90.

DAY SEVEN

 Store in your heart: Nahum 1:7

Read and discuss: Nahum 1:1-15; 2:2,8,13; 3:4-7,19

QUESTIONS FOR DISCUSSION OR INDIVIDUAL STUDY

- ∞ Discuss what you learned about Nineveh in Nahum.

- ∞ What relationship exists between Nineveh and Judah? What do they have in common?

- ∞ What do you learn about God in Nahum?

- ∞ How does this compare to what you learned about God in Hosea and Micah?

- ∞ What hope is there for Judah?

- ∞ What can you apply to your lives from Nahum?

THOUGHT FOR THE WEEK

There was once a television commercial about a butter substitute that tasted so much like butter it fooled everyone, "even Mother Nature." When the truth that it wasn't butter came out, thunder sounded and lightning struck from the heavens. The commercial ended with the line, "It's not nice to fool Mother Nature!"

From the beginning, people have suffered from the similar delusions that they can fool God and not experience bad consequences for their behavior. Sometimes they assume that since they *haven't* been punished they *never will be;* they mistake God's *stay* of execution for *vindication.* Nothing is further from the truth.

When Jonah predicted God's judgment on Nineveh, the king and people repented, and God stayed execution. Years later, Assyria returned to its evil ways, essentially thumbing its nose at God's kindness. Somewhere in between, the revival in Jonah's day burned out. Judgment came.

Repenting "for a limited time only" is no guarantee that an individual or nation will escape God's wrath. The only way to escape God's wrath is through permanent faith in the gospel, faith in Jesus Christ.

The world does not accept the notion of a God that judges. Insurers call hurricanes, tsunamis, floods, fires, earthquakes, and tornados "acts of *God*" to limit their liabilities, but no one interprets this to mean more than "situations *beyond our control.*" People may laugh at a vindictive Mother Nature in a commercial, but they're repulsed by any serious idea of a sovereign Judge who will call them to account for moral offenses.

If Assyria had known God as the just Judge He is, and Israel and Judah as the apple of His eye, would they have attacked His chosen people? Probably not! Because they didn't have this knowledge, God used them to judge Israel's sin—His motive was good; theirs was bad. (For this sharp difference between God's and the Assyrians' motives *in the same act,* see Isaiah 10:5-7,12-19. See also Genesis 50:20 for the general principle.)

How does this apply to us? Have you ever felt completely secure, no longer vulnerable to the contingencies of life, safe from the schemes of others, and able to decide right from wrong for yourself? What makes you feel this way?

Has anyone living this way ever gotten away with it in the long run? How does this kind of life mesh with what you know about God?

Think about what you learned from Nahum that can help you warn people that God must judge sin. Think of how Nahum's oracle begins—with God: who He is and what His character demands. Have you ever thought about approaching people this way? Think through how Nahum presents God. How will that help you confront sin when you need to?

Jonah preached judgment, and Nineveh repented. Nahum preached judgment, and Nineveh was judged. You and I aren't responsible for response to truth; we're responsible only to declare it in love as Ephesians tells us. If we truly love the world as God does, we can't withhold truth. *He* never did.

NAHUM AT A GLANCE

Theme of Nahum:

SEGMENT DIVISIONS

Author:

		CHAPTER THEMES
		1
		2
		3

Date:

Purpose:

Key Words:
Judah

God

Nineveh (and
all references
to it)

harlotry

nations

ZEPHANIAH

INTRODUCTION TO ZEPHANIAH

Zephaniah came preaching at the beginning of young King Josiah's reign. Josiah's great-grandfather was Hezekiah, a godly king of Judah who led reforms and witnessed a revival. Hezekiah and the prophet Isaiah turned to God when Assyria attacked Judah, and God turned Assyria away. But afterward Hezekiah's son Manasseh ruled wickedly for 55 years, and Manasseh's son Amon followed suit.

So how would Josiah reign? Whose example would he follow? God sent Zephaniah to preach during this time. What effect would this prophet have on Josiah?

WHAT DOES THE FUTURE HOLD?

∾∾∾∾∾

When a storm has passed and you begin to survey the landscape, looking at devastation around you, life can look pretty hopeless. It's hard to figure out where to begin—the tasks of cleaning up and rebuilding look so big, so difficult, or maybe even impossible. This is when you need someone to come along and help you see future possibilities. Zephaniah stepped onto the scene after the long devastating reign of wicked King Manasseh in Judah. He helped King Josiah see possible futures.

DAY ONE

Read Zephaniah 1 today, marking *I will* and *the day of the Lord*. Optionally you can mark other references to *the Lord*. Also double underline all geographical locations.

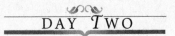

DAY TWO

As you saw yesterday while marking Zephaniah 1, the day of the Lord is an important topic in Zephaniah. You'll see this in the next two chapters as well. This is a significant day throughout the Bible.

Notice where you marked *I will* and list everything the Lord is planning to do.

What is the day of the Lord called in verses 8 and 18?

Now look over your work and think through the 5 W's and an H questions that your lists answer.

Record a theme for Zephaniah 1 on ZEPHANIAH AT A GLANCE on page 99.

DAY THREE

Read Zephaniah 2 today and mark *the day of the Lord, remnant,*[1] *desolation,*[2] time references, and geographical locations. *Assyria* and *Nineveh* are mentioned in this chapter, so mark them as you did in Nahum. (If you're consistent, you'll easily spot the references.)

DAY FOUR

Compare Zephaniah 2:2-3 to Zephaniah 1:8,18. Are the descriptions consistent?

What will happen to Assyria and Nineveh? What does this tell you about the timing of Zephaniah's ministry compared to Nahum's?

What other nations are mentioned, and what will happen to them?

Is there any hope for Israel or Judah?

Determine the theme of Zephaniah 2 and record it on ZEPHANIAH AT A GLANCE on page 99.

DAY FIVE

Read Zephaniah 3 today, marking the same key words you did before: *the day of the Lord, remnant,*[3] *I will,* and time and geographical references. Also mark *the nations.*

Read verses 1-7 again, which contain a reference to "the tyrannical city." Can you identify the city? Uniquely mark all references to her, then read the rest of the chapter to see if she is mentioned again.

DAY SIX

Add what you learned about *the day of the Lord* to the information you recorded earlier in the week.

What will happen to the nations?

What do you learn about the future of Israel?

Record a theme for Zephaniah 3 on ZEPHANIAH AT A GLANCE on page 99.

DAY SEVEN

Store in your heart: Zephaniah 1:7
Read and discuss: Zephaniah 1:7-9,14-18; 2:1-11;
3:11-20; Isaiah 13:6-16

QUESTIONS FOR DISCUSSION OR INDIVIDUAL STUDY

- Discuss the day of the Lord—the who, what, when, where, why, and how.

- What is the future of the nations?

- What is Israel's future?

- How do Zephaniah and Nahum fit together?

- Discuss responses people have to this kind of message.

- What's your response to this message? What do you think you should do?

THOUGHT FOR THE WEEK

The day of the Lord is a day of judgment, anger, wrath... a terrible day. If you study *Discovering the God of Second Chances,* you'll see its importance in Joel, Amos, and Obadiah. If you study *Opening the Windows of Blessing,* you'll see its importance in Zechariah and Malachi. It is mentioned throughout the prophets and in seven New Testament books. Other Bible books simply refer to it as "that day."

Why is this subject so important? What relevance does it have for our lives and the lives of those around us?

If you care about people, you should care about the day of the Lord. If you believe the Bible is true, descriptions of the day of the Lord should cause you to fear for those who don't know Him, whether you know them or not.

The message was important enough for God to keep sending prophets to Israel right through New Testament times. He wants us to know so we'll take appropriate action. We need to do more than just change our thinking; we also need to live in the light of truth. And for other people, it's a matter of life and death because language about the coming wrath of God is not hyperbole (exaggeration); it's real stuff.

Where is hope in this?

God extends hope through His promise to those who seek righteousness. Zephaniah 2:1-3 says we are to gather ourselves *before* the day of the Lord's anger to seek righteousness and humility—perhaps we'll be hidden. Hope is found in the promise that the Lord will care for the remnant and restore their fortunes. It's found in the promise that a humble people who take refuge in the name of the Lord will survive. They will feed and lie down with no one to make them tremble.

These promises are rooted in the character of God—His faithfulness to those He establishes covenants with. And they're designed to show hope beyond certain and immediate judgment. And God's character and Word reveal that this hope extends beyond Israel.

We can look beyond Zephaniah, beyond the Old Testament, to the New Testament, and find hope there for our day too—for us, our family, our friends, our neighbors, and others in our community who are not Israel. First Thessalonians 4:13–5:11 tells us we should *not* be like those who have no hope. We know that those who have fallen asleep in Christ (the saved who have died) will rise, and we who are alive at that time will be caught up together with them to meet the Lord in the air and then always be with the Lord. We have these words to comfort those who believe.

And what about those who haven't believed? They need to hear the bad news and the good news, wrath and grace, judgment and mercy. If they don't respond in faith to this news, the day of the Lord will come upon them like a thief in the night, and they will not escape.

Those who believe are not destined for wrath, but those who do not believe will bear the full consequences of their sin. Those who believe don't bear *these* consequences, because Jesus bore this penalty on the cross for them. There's hope—hope in the cross. Our hope is in believing this gospel.

And as Peter tells us in 2 Peter 3:15, we should regard the patience of the Lord as salvation, for each day we have until the day of the Lord is another day someone can hear and believe the gospel. Every day the Lord tarries is a day of grace, a day of hope.

In this we should rejoice, be grateful, and be diligent to live in light of the patience of the Lord, making the most of our time, "redeeming" it as Ephesians 5:16 and Colossians 4:5 urge us to do.

And most of all, we should hope in the sure and steadfast anchor the living God has given to our souls.

Theme of Zephaniah:

SEGMENT
DIVISIONS

CHAPTER THEMES

Author:

Date:

Purpose:

Key Words:

I will (the Lord
will, He will)

the day of the
Lord (the day, in
or on that day)

remnant
(remainder)

every reference
to God's people,
nation (daughters
of Zion)

nations
(kingdoms,
peoples)

desolation

HABAKKUK

INTRODUCTION TO HABAKKUK

Though Habakkuk's prophecy is positioned before Zephaniah's in the Bible, Habakkuk was probably the last prophet to minister before the Babylonian captivity of Judah, the last messenger God sent to turn His people back. Through him, God revealed to them the judgment He brought, yet He also gave them a simple truth to hope in: "The righteous shall live by faith."

Why, God?

The righteous shall live by faith. Romans, Galatians, and Hebrews all echo Habakkuk's original message, which struck Martin Luther like a lightning bolt, giving rise to the Protestant Reformation. And since then, the same message has given hope to everyone enslaved to works—people never able to do enough, never able to reach the ideal, never able to understand why bad things happen to good people.

DAY ONE

Read Habakkuk 1, marking references to *Habakkuk, the nations,* the *Chaldeans, wickedness,*[1] and the *Lord.* As always, it's good to make a bookmark with these so you can mark key words consistently throughout a book of the Bible.

DAY TWO

What did you learn from marking *Habakkuk* and the *Chaldeans?* What is Habakkuk's dilemma?

What do you learn from marking *God* and *wickedness?*

How does God relate to the Chaldeans? What role do they play in His plans?

Record a theme for Habakkuk 1 on HABAKKUK AT A GLANCE on page 110.

DAY THREE

Let's continue our quest to understand God's message through Habakkuk by reading Habakkuk 2 today, marking the key words from your bookmark. Add *vision*,[2] *faith, woe,* and *idol*.[3]

DAY FOUR

Add what you learned in chapter 2 about *Habakkuk* and the *Chaldeans* to the list you made earlier this week.

What did you learn from marking *vision?*

Look up Romans 1:16-17; Galatians 3:11; and Hebrews 10:38; and compare them to Habakkuk 2:4.

The Hebrew word translated "faith" in Habakkuk 2:4 means firm, steadfast, steady, trustworthy, dependable. The Greek equivalent in the three New Testament verses includes the ideas of reliance, trust, and assurance.

Read Hebrews 11:1-6 and list what you learn about faith.

According to Ephesians 2:8-10, what role does faith play in salvation?

Whom are the righteous contrasted with in Habakkuk 2?

DAY FIVE

What do you learn from marking *woes* in Habakkuk 2? Answer the 5 W's and an H.

And what do you learn from marking *idols?*

What do you learn about the Lord from this chapter? How does this help you understand what He's doing?

Don't forget to determine the theme of Habakkuk 2 and record it on HABAKKUK AT A GLANCE on page 110.

DAY SIX

Read Habakkuk 3 today, marking the key words from your bookmark.

How does Habakkuk 3 begin? What does Habakkuk ask for? Why?

How does Habakkuk end? What is his reaction to all he has learned about God?

Record a theme for Habakkuk 3 on HABAKKUK AT A GLANCE on page 110.

DAY SEVEN

 Store in your heart: Habakkuk 3:17-19

Read and discuss: Habakkuk 1:1-6,12; 2:1-5,18-20; 3:1-7,16-19; Romans 1:16-17

QUESTIONS FOR DISCUSSION OR INDIVIDUAL STUDY

- ✺ Have you ever questioned God, asked "why?" or wondered where He was in unjust situations? What do you think of such questions now?

- ✺ Discuss the dialog (questions and answers) between Habakkuk and God. Analyze Habakkuk's response to God's answers.

- ✺ Have you ever raised the same questions? What answers did you find?

- ✺ Discuss God's instructions to Habakkuk in chapter 2. What application can you make to your life? What's your responsibility?

- ✺ What do you base your salvation on? Do you live daily by faith? If not, what's stopping you?

- ✺ What have you learned from this study that will impact your life? How will it affect your relationship with Almighty God?

THOUGHT FOR THE WEEK

Has there ever been a time in your life when you questioned God? Possibly you found yourself in a situation you never dreamed would happen. Maybe you cried for help and God seemed not to hear. You weren't delivered. You suffered. Life seemed dark.

When you go through these things, do you wonder where God is? If He's in charge of this universe, why does He let the world continue on a course to self-destruction? Why doesn't He stop cruel and bizarre things from happening in the world?

Maybe you know something that happened to a child of God that was so unjust, so evil, that you doubt God's compassion. You wonder how God can allow such things to happen, but you don't verbalize such thoughts for fear that you'll appear unholy. Have you ever wondered where God is when bad things happen?

Habakkuk not only wondered, he also verbalized these thoughts. But rather than condemning him, God answered his doubts.

And His answer was challenging. He said that He was doing something Habakkuk would not believe even if He told him. Perhaps that's part of our problem—we won't believe God's answer because it's not what we expect, want, or understand.

Sometimes God's *ways* are hard to understand; that's what He told Habakkuk. But God's *character* is not hard to understand. He has revealed Himself so clearly in His Word that if we diligently seek Him there, we'll understand. If we can understand His patience to be the open door to salvation for those who have not yet come to Him, perhaps we'll understand. Tragedies are one mechanism to draw people through that door.

In the 1950s, five missionaries dared to contact a native tribe, the Huaoranis, in the jungles of Ecuador. This tribe was notoriously savage, and killing was a way of life for them. In fact, other tribes called them the Aucas, which means "savage." But these missionaries wanted them to know about Jesus. When these missionaries had faced other hostile natives, they had been able to scare them away simply by firing guns in the air.

Nate Saint was the missionary pilot who would fly the team into the remote jungle area. His son, Steve, asked him if he would shoot a native who was trying to kill him. Nate replied that if it came to taking a native's life to save his own, he wouldn't because he knew the man wouldn't be ready for heaven…and he was.

Nate and the four other missionaries, including Jim Elliot, made contact with the Huaoranis in January of 1956. A few days later, the natives attacked, spearing the missionaries, who had fired their guns into the air to no avail. All five missionaries died shortly after. The Huaoranis lived on in their sins, but one day they would hear the gospel and believe, readying themselves for heaven.

Young Steve struggled to understand why his father died. But harder still for him was understanding why the murderers should live. How can such a bad thing happen to such a good person? How can good things happen to the bad? In short, how can such injustices go on? The missionaries' experience seemed like a complete inversion—the good punished and the wicked rewarded.

But one day Jim Elliot's wife, Elisabeth, went back, and God saved many of the Auca Indians. And He has used this story to inspire thousands of men and women to enter missionary service. When *Life* magazine first featured the story, a new generation of missionary-minded people was created. The five missionaries wanted to give the gospel to this fierce tribe. Elisabeth Elliot and others honored that original vision, as many others have since.

We can easily lose sight of God's eternal purposes when we focus on the world's perception of bad things. Too often, like the world, we live our lives in the here and now, forgetting that God's eternal purposes not only are never thwarted by man's evil but also actually encompass it, accomplishing His good desires.

Thus it has been since man's fall (Genesis 3:15). When life seems dark, we find hope in God.

Theme of Habakkuk:

SEGMENT
DIVISIONS

Author:

CHAPTER THEMES

Date:

Purpose:

Key Words:

Chaldeans

wickedness

the Lord

vision

faith

woe

idol

HOSEA

1. KJV; ESV: whoredom; NIV: adulterous, unfaithfulness
2. KJV: mercies; NKJV; ESV: mercy
3. NIV: prostitute; ESV: whore
4. KJV: whoredom; NIV: prostitution; ESV: whore
5. KJV: whoredoms; NIV: prostitution; ESV: whore
6. KJV; ESV: whoredom; NIV: prostitution
7. NIV: acknowledgement
8. KJV: goodness; NIV: love; NKJV: faithfulness
9. KJV; NIV; NKJV; ESV: mercy
10. KJV; NIV; ESV: as
11. KJV; NKJV: Gentiles
12. KJV; NKJV: backsliding
13. NIV; NKJV: repent
14. NIV: treaty

MICAH

1. KJV: evil; NIV; NKJV; ESV: disaster
2. NIV: calamity; ESV: disaster
3. NIV: ruined
4. KJV; ESV: house
5. KJV: people
6. KJV: controversy; NIV: accusation; NKJV: complaint
7. KJV; NIV; NKJV: mercy

NAHUM

1. KJV: whoredoms; NIV: wanton lust, prostitution; ESV: whorings

ZEPHANIAH

1. KJV; NKJV; ESV; NIV: survivors
2. NIV: left in ruins, rubble, ruin; ESV: devastation
3. ESV: those who are left

HABAKKUK

1. KJV: grievance, iniquity; NIV: injustice, wrong; NKJV; ESV: wrong
2. NIV: revelation
3. KJV: graven image; NKJV: image

BOOKS IN THE
NEW INDUCTIVE STUDY SERIES